THE SLAVE TRADE

Nigel Sadler

SHIRE PUBLICATIONS

First published in Great Britain in 2009 by Shire
Publications Ltd, Midland House, West Way, Botley,
Oxford OX2 0PH, United Kingdom.

443 Park Avenue South, New York, NY 10016, USA.

E-mail: shire@shirebooks.co.uk   www.shirebooks.co.uk

A CIP catalogue record for this book is available from the
British Library.

Shire Library no. 485   •   ISBN-13: 978 0 7478 0708 7

Nigel Sadler has asserted his right under the Copyright,
Designs and Patents Act, 1988, to be identified as the
author of this book.

Designed by Ken Vail Graphic Design, Cambridge, UK and
typeset in Perpetua and Gill Sans.
Printed in China through Worldprint

09 10 11 12 13   10 9 8 7 6 5 4 3 2 1

COVER IMAGE
Slave market in Charleston, South Carolina, 1856.

TITLE PAGE IMAGE
Enslaved Africans on board a ship.

CONTENTS PAGE IMAGE
Enslaved workers cutting sugar cane, Antigua 1823.

DEDICATION
This book is dedicated to all those who suffered as
enslaved workers and to all who fought against the unjust
system.

ACKNOWLEDGEMENTS
I would like to thank my parents, Paul and Elizabeth
Sadler, who instilled in me an interest in the past; to the
Museums Association of the Caribbean who first
stimulated my desire to understand more about the
transatlantic slave trade and its legacy; and to Val Munday
and Enfield Museum Service who inspired the original
research for an exhibition.

PHOTOGRAPHIC CREDITS
Tony Aitman, Black Voices, Liverpool, page 39;
Bridgeman Art Library, contents page (© British Library
Board. All rights reserved), and pages 6 (© Heini
Schneebeli), and 30 (private collection); © Enfield
Museum Service (Photo by Simon O'Connor) page 57;
Library of Congress page 46.

All other images are from the collections of Sands of Time
Consultancy

CONTENTS

INTRODUCTION

Iᴺ the early fifteenth century a quest for new resources and trade routes to the Far East brought Europeans to West Africa. It was during these explorations that the wealth of the region was discovered and soon explorers and traders started to bring gold, ivory and a limited number of enslaved Africans back to Europe. However, the potential for exploitation of human resources was not fully realised until the Europeans discovered the Americas in 1492.

When the European nations, especially Britain, France, Spain and Portugal, started their colonial expansions in the sixteenth and seventeenth centuries they needed labour to sustain their developing empires.

Inspecting an enslaved African before boarding a slave ship.

The greatest demand for labour came from the plantations, the large farms or estates that developed in the New World, which concentrated on growing a single crop, usually cotton, tobacco, coffee, sugar cane, cocoa or rice. As cities and towns grew in the Americas there was a corresponding need for domestic workers. These labour demands were to be met by enslaving Africans; thus, slavery became part of all levels of the economy and the transatlantic slave trade was born.

Branding an African before sending him to a slave ship.

Britain was eventually to become dominant in the transatlantic slave trade, and the first known British trader in Africans was John Hawkins. Between 1562 and 1567, Hawkins made four journeys between the Sierra Leone River and Hispaniola (modern-day Haiti and the Dominican Republic), taking a total of 1,200 enslaved Africans to sell to the Spanish settlers. Paradoxically, after dominating the slave trade for over two hundred years, Britain later became a leading nation in its abolition.

This book looks at the transatlantic slave trade, which lasted for over three hundred years between the sixteenth and nineteenth centuries, and explores its legacies.

AFRICA AND ENSLAVEMENT

A T THE START of the transatlantic slave trade Africa was a continent of numerous cultures with well-developed political and religious systems in place. However, instead of recognising this wealth of diversity, early European explorers depicted the Africans as pagan savages – for many, this provided adequate justification for their interference.

THE WEST COAST

The most interesting part of Africa for the European nations was the West Coast, and here they traded with many different states: the Mali Empire, with its capital at Timbuktu, which became a centre for arts and crafts and a major Islamic settlement, influencing West Africa; the Bambaran state, which rose out of the decline of Timbuktu in the early eighteenth century; and Oyo (founded in around 1400 as one of the Yoruba, a collection of autonomous kingdoms in modern-day Nigeria), which took control of the River Niger to gain access inland to new resources and slaves. Also of interest to European traders were Dahomey (one of the Oyo states that rose to power in the early nineteenth century); the kingdom of Benin (1470–1897), which was renowned for the skills of its artisans; and the Ashanti, one of the Akan states in modern-day Ghana, which became one of the greatest empires in West Africa, dominating trade in gold and slaves.

For ease of identification, the Europeans designated the areas of the West Coast of Africa stretching from modern-day Ivory Coast to Nigeria by the types of trade that were expected – the Ivory Coast, the Gold Coast and the Slave Coast. These simplified regional names indicated the main reason why European nations were here: to exploit the natural resources. Once Europeans had discovered the trade potential of West Africa, the fate of the Africans was sealed. Greed and ruthless efficiency saw the Europeans fighting for control, making alliances with African kings and building forts for protection.

A HISTORY OF ENSLAVEMENT

Slavery was not a new phenomenon in Africa. Before the start of the transatlantic slave trade many African societies utilised slave labour. Some sold

Opposite:
Plaque that once adorned wooden pillars of the Benin royal palace, c. sixteenth century. The Portuguese figure on the right holds a manilla, a form of currency used to purchase enslaved Africans.

Coronation of the
King of Whidah,
c.1795.

members of their community that they wanted to get rid of (such as criminals, people with mental illness and troublesome youths) to pay debts to other tribes. Other Africans were kidnapped whilst going about their daily duties or during raids on their villages, but the majority were captured through wars that were fought over many issues. In Africa in most cases the enslaved could rise to a position of power and grow wealthy – their title of 'slave' often did not limit their potential. However, the Europeans took slavery to an unimaginable level, and dehumanised the victims, removing all their rights.

Bottom: Village on
the banks of the
River Niger.

EUROPEAN INVOLVEMENT

The European transatlantic slave trade increased demand for enslaved Africans, and tribal conflict now served as an excuse to capture slaves. Even though the Europeans created demand for enslaved workers, it was often Africans who sold fellow Africans into slavery. Some tribes became very efficient at capturing Africans through war or kidnap and started to go further afield to gather people to meet the demands. This meant that the captured Africans had greater distances to walk before being sold to the Europeans. Ottobah Cugoano,

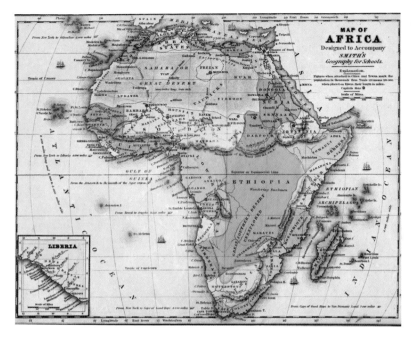

Left: Africa, 1839, just after Britain abolished slavery in its territories.

Below left: Accra Market, c.1910. The African marketplace had changed little over the centuries. Captains and sailors of slave ships would purchase items at the local markets hoping to sell them in the Americas or Europe for large profit, to supplement their low incomes.

remembering his capture, wrote in 1787, 'I was early snatched away from my native country, with about eighteen or twenty more boys and girls, as we were playing in a field. Some of us attempted, in vain, to run away, but the pistols and cutlasses were soon introduced, threatening if we offered to stir, we should all lie dead on the spot.'

Below right: A slave hunter.

9

THE TRIANGULAR TRADE

FROM EUROPE TO AFRICA

SLAVERY existed as part of a more complex trading network linking Europe, Africa and the Americas. This three-legged trade route became better known as the 'Triangular Trade'. The first leg saw slave ships loaded with trade products sailing from Europe to Africa. Amongst the items exported were guns and gunpowder; however, giving potential enemies the means to resist was not a good business move so in most cases the guns were of poor quality. Other items became standard currency such as cowrie shells from the Indian Ocean, glass beads, often made in Italy, iron rods or bars, and copper and bronze bracelets known as manillas. These manillas became a sign of the slave trade and could be worn as personal adornment, were melted down in Africa to create art and religious figures, or were used as money, remaining a currency in some parts until the 1950s. Alcohol was also exported and used to help smooth out the negotiation process to purchase the enslaved. The nineteenth-century slave trader Theodore Canot recorded that 'prices had already been arranged with the quick for what quantity of each goods a female, male and child slave would raise'.

The slave ships also carried passengers from Europe, but of course they did not travel in the same cramped conditions as the Africans later would on their journey. These passengers were often replacement staff and soldiers for the forts and administration centres, or individual entrepreneurs looking to make their fortune in Africa or the Americas. There were also personal or business-related items sent out from Europe to companies and family members in the Caribbean, South America or North America.

FROM AFRICA TO THE AMERICAS

The second leg of the 'Triangular Trade' predominantly saw enslaved people being taken to the Americas. After their forced march the captured Africans (those who had survived the whippings, beatings and rape) were placed into a slave warehouse, also known as a trunk. Initially owned by the king or officials of the local tribes, these warehouses later became managed by slave traders. Conditions in these warehouses were horrific. When purchasing

Opposite:
The captured Africans had to walk to the coast, in some cases for many hundreds of miles.

Many died or were murdered on the walk, and women often suffered physical and sexual abuse. Food and water were also in short supply, often leading to starvation and death. If the captors risked starvation they would abandon the enslaved Africans.

Africans at Whidaw (in modern-day Benin), Captain Phillips of the slave ship *Hannibal* recorded in 1693 that he 'often fainted with the horrid stink of the negroes, it being an old house where all the slaves are kept together, and evacuate nature where they lie, so that no jakes can stink worse; there being forced to sit three or four hours at a time, quite ruined my health'.

The Europeans started on a small scale by trading with local villages. However, as profits increased European countries needed to protect their trade and built forts. The best-known slave fort, Elmina Castle, in modern-day Ghana, was built in 1482 by the Portuguese and seized by the Dutch in 1637.

Slave post where enslaved Africans were gathered together for sale.

A slave shed in the Congo.

The enslaved Africans were led through the castle's infamous 'door of no return' to board the slave ships. Over the next three centuries the English, Dutch, Swedes, Danes, French and even the German Duchy of Brandenburg joined the Portuguese in setting up castles and forts along the coast to trade with the interior states. Some of the earliest British forts were built or managed by the Royal African Company who held the British monopoly in the Atlantic slave trade between 1672 and 1698 and needed to protect their trade. They kept the purchased Africans in these forts before sending them onto their ships bound for the Americas.

Cape Coast Castle, shown here in the late nineteenth century, was built by the Swedish in 1653 and captured by the British in 1664. It became a symbol of British control in the area.

During the purchasing and loading process, the enslaved Africans were carefully monitored by the ship's doctor to ensure that they had no visible signs of disease. After purchase the Africans would be taken from the slave fort or slave warehouse to waiting canoes that carried them to the ship. Many tried to jump to freedom before being taken down to the ship's hold but those who succeeded in escaping often drowned. Whilst the slave ship was anchored off the coast of Africa some of the enslaved faced further hardships: they could spend several months in the ship's hold waiting as the captain continued to purchase Africans.

Slave trader Theodore Canot recorded, 'After receiving the slave they then mark'd the slaves we had bought in the breast or shoulder, with a hot iron, having the letter of the ship's name on it.'

The journey across the Atlantic is better known as the 'Middle Passage', but this sees the trade from a European viewpoint, and the term 'transatlantic passage' is preferred by many. To keep the Africans alive it was essential that the ships were well stocked with food and water, which took up a considerable amount of storage space. To make the ship's journey as profitable as possible, a large quantity of gold and ivory was loaded as well, much of this making its way back to Europe. Other items depended on the changing tastes of the markets and included things such as African cloth and metalwork to be sold in the Caribbean or Europe.

Captured Africans being carried to a slave ship in a canoe.

Life on the slave ships was horrific, as the tightly packed human cargo could remain in these cramped conditions for two or three months. Limited sanitation meant disease was rife and the smell of human suffering was overpowering, best described by Olaudah Equiano who, in 1789, recalled, 'I was soon put down under the decks, and there I received such a salutation in my nostrils as I had never experienced in my life.' Sailors could smell an approaching slave ship from 5 miles away. In the hold the enslaved Africans died where they lay, their bodies remaining chained to fellow Africans, sometimes for days. A quarter of the estimated twelve million Africans loaded for the Americas died during the transatlantic crossing.

The captains of some ships protected the Africans from abuse and unwarranted punishment, and made sure they gained regular exercise and were fed frequently. Some did this for moral reasons, others for financial

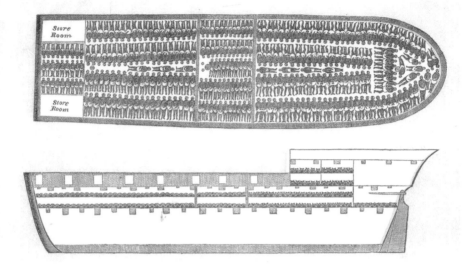

Above: Thomas Clarkson prepared a drawing of the slave ship *Brookes* to show the conditions the Africans suffered during the Atlantic crossing.

Map opposite: The Caribbean (1830s) after the end of slavery in British territories.

reasons. (The better the enslaved Africans were treated, the more chance they would arrive healthier and make a bigger profit.) Unfortunately, many captains just loaded the ships as fully as possible and gave no consideration to the conditions of the enslaved. It is no surprise, therefore, that one in ten slave ships suffered a revolt. Often this was violently stopped by the crew and any disobedience was treated harshly. This included whipping them, cutting off limbs and even throwing the Africans into the sea to drown. There were also individual acts of resistance, the most extreme being enslaved Africans committing suicide or killing their young infants by throwing them into the sea.

THE RETURN JOURNEY

The final leg of the triangular trade saw the slave ships, loaded with produce from the Caribbean, South America and North America, returning to Britain. These products were purchased using the revenue from the sale of the enslaved Africans or with gold purchased in Africa. Initially, many items shipped to Europe were to meet the needs of the more wealthy citizens. Eventually though, as trade increased and prices fell, these products became available to a wider market. These bulky items included sugar, coffee, cocoa, cotton and tobacco. For example, coffee houses grew in popularity; cocoa, originally introduced for medicinal uses, became a popular drink when sweetened with sugar; and the mills in northern England prized the imported cotton because of its quality and low cost.

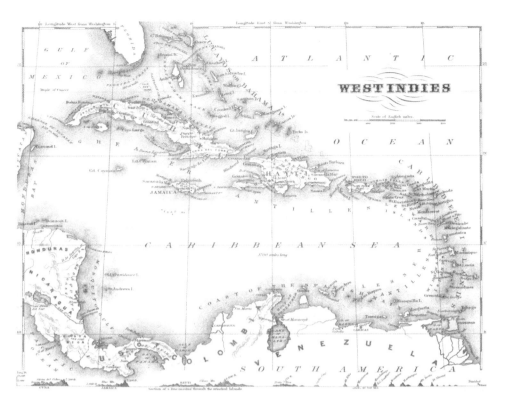

Many European plantation owners often spent little or no time in the Americas. They used the profits to build up a grand lifestyle in Europe, with big houses and important positions in society. To maintain this status they would ship luxury items such as turtle meat back to Europe, and these items would be produced at parties as proof of the plantation owners' standing.

Below left: Jamaican sugar cane cutters.

Below right: Cotton production.

For Sale,

A NEGRO WENCH, about 22 years of age, a goo[d] Plain Cook Washer and Ironer; sober, hone[st] and no runaway; sold for no fault, her present own[er] having no use for her. For terms apply to

Wm Stephens,

April 10.　　　　3　　　　*Beale's Wharf*

PUBLIC AUCTION.
—

*On TUESDAY the 6th May next, immediately after t[he]
sale of Canal shares, will be sold.*

A LL that valuable LOT, with the buildings thereo[n] situated in Meeting street at the corner of B[e]resford's alley, well known as *M'Leans Tavern and g[ro]cery store.* The Lot contains 39 feet front on Meetin[g] street, by 32 feet deep on Beresfords alley. The buildings are roomy and convenient, and is considered [an] excellent stand for the above business.

—— ALSO ——

A NEGRO FELLOW named WASHINGTON.

The above being the property of the estate of Eve[r] M'Lean, deceased, and sold by order of the executors. *Conditions* — Notes with approved indorsers, payable [in] 6, 9 and 12 months, with a mortgage of the property.

William Payne.

April 9.

Blank Bills of Lading,

THE SLAVE MARKET

UPON ARRIVAL in the New World the Africans who had been purchased in advance went straight to the plantations and were spared the slave market experience. However, the vast majority of new arrivals would have been sent to the market to be sold. The dehumanising aspect of slavery was apparent at the slave markets: they were set up in a similar fashion to those for livestock. The enslaved were treated like animals; they were handled, pinched, hit, inspected, and intimate examinations were undertaken in public. First-generation Africans fresh from the slave ships were oiled up to make them look healthier, and old rags were used to conceal any evidence of dysentery or diarrhoea.

Slave markets also developed for the internal trade requirements. Some planters fell on hard times and needed to sell their enslaved workers, whilst others had too many enslaved workers. Also, when planters died, their assets, including the enslaved labour, were sold off. These markets also dealt with those who had already lived as enslaved workers in the New World for whatever reason. Mary Prince recalled the day she went to the slave market in Bermuda to be sold to raise funds to pay for her owner's wedding.

Family life was restricted and the threat of family break-up was high due to the selling of children and movement of enslaved workers between plantations irrespective of family ties. Following the end of the importation of Africans after 1807 in British territories (1808 in the USA and at various other dates for the rest of the New World), slave owners realised the importance of stronger family ties. Without stable family life there would be fewer children and the enslaved population would decline. The enslaved had to have children to maintain their numbers. However, every type of auction, either for the newly arrived Africans or for those already enslaved in the New World, often led to the splitting up of families. In the USA, Martha Browne recalled the day she was sold and separated from her mother: 'A tall, hard-looking man came up to me, very roughly seized my arm, bade me open my mouth; examined my teeth; felt of my limbs; made me run a few yards; ordered me to jump; and, being well satisfied with my activity, said to Master Edward, "I will take her." [My mother] gave full vent to her feelings in a long, loud, piteous wail.'

Opposite:
Newspaper advert
for the sale of
slaves in
Charleston, 1806.

KNOW ALL MEN BY THESE PRESENTS,

THAT WE *John S. Morrow & Francis Morrow* are held and firmly bound unto the Branch of the Bank of the State of Alabama at Decatur

in the penal sum of *three thousand five hundred and ninety six* dollars and *83¼* cents, which payment well and truly to be made, we bind ourselves and each of our heirs firmly by these presents, sealed with our seals and dated this *7* day of *December* 1841

THE CONDITION OF THE ABOVE OBLIGATION IS SUCH, That whereas CHRISTOPHER C. GEWIN, Sheriff of Lawrence County, Alabama, hath by virtue of a writ of fieri facias issued out of the *Circuit* Court of said County on the *4* day of *November* 1841 against the goods and chattels, lands and tenements of the above bounden *Patrick Neal Wm H Price & Thomas Person* at the suit of the above mentioned *Branch of the Bank State of Alabama at Decatur* for the sum of *thirteen* hundred *& 58* dollars and *5 5/7* cents debt, *and four hundred & sixteen* dollars and *61¼* cents damages, and *twenty three* dollars and *2 5/7* cents cost of suit—returnable three days previous to the *third* Monday in *March next* levied on the following goods and chattels of the above bounden *Wm H. Price* to wit *one negro woman Maria about 25 years old one negro girl Patience about 6 years old and one girl Emily 3 or four years old all levied on as the property of William H. Price*

NOW If the above bounden *John S Morrow* procure and deliver the above named goods and chattels to the said Sheriff or proper officer at *Courtland* on the day of *January* 1842 at 12 o'clock noon, on that day, being the time appointed for sale of the above mentioned goods and chattels, then this obligation to be void, otherwise to remain in full force and virtue.—Signed and sealed in presence of

Charles Gibson

John S Morrow

Right: Slave market at St Augustine, Florida.

Opposite: This summons to retrieve debts (Lawrence County, Alabama, 1842) shows John Morrow's debt being levied on his property, his slaves. It is possible that these slaves were sold to meet his debt.

> **Wanted to purchase for cash.**
>
> A MIDDLE aged Negro WOMAN; a complete House Servant and seamstress, of warranted character. None else will answer. Enquire at No. 72 Broad-street.   July 6

Left: Newspaper advert requesting to purchase a domestic slave, Charleston 1822.

Below: An old slave block in New Orleans. The woman present was sold as a child from this block.

The slave markets were a very visible way of trading enslaved workers. However, the auctions charged commission and were an expensive way to sell or buy an enslaved worker, especially if it involved only one or two people. Therefore, some people used the local newspapers to offer for sale, or request a purchase, and it was not uncommon to see the sale of humans listed next to everyday items. There were also adverts that listed the ships arriving and their cargoes, sometimes including enslaved people, and promoting the place and date of the sale of these items.

WORKING LIFE

THE FIRST enslaved labourers in the Caribbean were not African. The Spanish tried to enslave the indigenous Amerindians but many died from diseases brought in by the Europeans or through overwork and there were insufficient numbers to meet the ever-increasing mining and production needs. Indentured labourers from Europe were also tried but they could not adapt to working in the extreme conditions so an alternative source of labour was needed.

PLANTATIONS

The development of the New World was based on a plantation economy, and everyone needed to know their place in society. The plantation owner managed the estate and, if he had a wife she managed the house and domestic enslaved labour. On larger plantations a white overseer supervised the field work and punishments, and if the plantation owner was absent a manager would have been appointed. Trusted enslaved workers became slave drivers, watching over the enslaved labourers, making sure they worked and enforcing punishments. At the bottom of society was the enslaved labourer with no rights.

Many male plantation owners had relationships with female slaves; quite often these were non-consensual. Slave owners could see no reason why they should not abuse these women either physically or sexually, as they were their property to do with as they pleased. Harriet Jacobs wrote in 1861, 'I now entered on my fifteenth year... He tried his utmost to corrupt the pure principles my grandmother had instilled... He told me I was his property; that I must be subject to his will in all things.' These liaisons often resulted in mixed-race children. Some slave owners ignored their illegitimate offspring, whilst others gave them trusted positions in the house. Unfortunately, by becoming domestic servants in the plantation house, these enslaved workers were brought into contact with the slave owner's wife, acting as a constant reminder of the husband's infidelity. This meant that in many houses the owner's wife treated the children from these liaisons with

Opposite:
Coffee plantation
in Brazil, 1850s.

Sugar plantation, Barbados, 1900, illustrating the landscape in which the enslaved worked.

Plantation owner's house, Pedro St James, Grand Cayman. Construction started in 1780 but the building had fallen into disrepair and has recently undergone reconstruction to create a tourist attraction.

Slave owner's grave, St Eustatius.

at best disdain, but at worst with brutality. Harriet Jacobs recalled that 'the mistress, who ought to protect the helpless victim, has no other feelings towards her but those of jealousy and rage'.

Newly imported enslaved Africans underwent 'seasoning' on the plantations for one to five years. This adapted them to life in slavery and trained them in the required tasks for use on the plantation. A third of all Africans died during 'seasoning' through disease or excessive punishment and in general life expectancy was low. On the Brazilian sugar plantations, for example, it was only eight years for enslaved labourers imported from Africa.

The main plantations in the Caribbean, USA and South America grew sugar, cotton, coffee, tobacco, rice and cocoa; areas were also set aside for crops and livestock to feed those living on the plantations. Generally, on cotton plantations the field labourers worked very long hours on whatever jobs needed to be done.

Coffee plantation in Brazil, 1850s.

Brazilian sugar mill, 1845.

Cotton production in the USA, 1850s.

On the coffee and cocoa plantations they worked a task system, where each worker was given a daily task and once it was finished they were free to do their own work, such as making produce for the market. On the plantations there were many areas of work and the labour was usually divided on the basis of age and physical ability. There were three levels of field work and types of worker to do them. The first did the heavy work, and were generally aged between 16 and 50. The second level was lighter work carried out by the young enslaved aged between 12 and 16, the ill, pregnant women and new mothers. The final gang did the weeding and clearing fields of small items and consisted mostly of children under the age of 12, often supervised by older trusted women. In addition to the field workers, many other enslaved workers were required to run a plantation: skilled labourers such as blacksmiths and carpenters were needed to maintain the tools and buildings, while domestic workers in the main house took care of cleaning, washing and cooking for the plantation owner and his family.

SLAVE LABOUR OUTSIDE THE PLANTATIONS

Plantation work may be the best-known form of enslaved labour, but in reality enslaved workers would have been used in every aspect of daily life. In the seventeenth century, gold mining became the main economy in Brazil, generating wealth that led to the development of towns and increasing demand for enslaved urban workers. This was true for all the New World and as the region developed the towns grew. Enslaved workers could be found in the homes working as cooks, seamstresses, maids, cleaners and wet nurses, breastfeeding the children of their slave masters. Many became skilled craftsmen such as builders, blacksmiths and carpenters, and were hired out for whatever duties a city needed. Not all domestic slaves had easier lives than the labourers. Washerwomen and water carriers, for example, worked

Enslaved workers were used as domestic servants in the cities.

as hard as the field labourers and suffered physical punishment if the work was not satisfactory. Many were also expected to work in the fields, especially at harvest time. Even children had jobs, including acting as companions to the young of the slave owners.

In some cases the enslaved were able to produce their own food or craft items during their free time for the family and market. The market became a vital place for community and social life because rules for congregation were relaxed and here the enslaved could gather news, learning about family members or even planning uprisings. It was even possible for some to meet up with friends and family who had been sold to other plantations. Slave owners often turned a blind eye to what happened at the market, as they were fearful that any interference might lead to disturbances or rebellion.

It was not just men who owned the enslaved. Some women built up their own plantations and others inherited estates from deceased husbands, were

Market in Haiti, c.1900. The marketplace had changed little from the days of slavery.

given enslaved workers as gifts or purchased their own workers to carry out their own small ventures, independently from their husbands. Women could be just as brutal when it came to punishing indiscretions. Mary Prince stated, '[my mistress] caused me to know the exact difference between the smart of the rope, the cart-whip, and the cow-skin, when applied to my naked body by her own cruel hand. And there was scarcely any punishment more dreadful than the blows I received on my face and head from her hard, heavy fist. She was a fearful woman, and a savage mistress to her slaves.'

LABOUR IN EUROPE

In Europe, where a large cheap labour force was readily available to work in the factories and in agriculture, there was no need to employ enslaved labour. The poem 'Rule, Britannia' by James Thomson (1700–48), put to music by Thomas Augustine Arne (c.1740), suggested that no Briton could be a slave. However, laws in England and Wales were ambiguous, and instead of being slaves many Africans were domestic labourers with limited rights, and if returned to the Caribbean would be placed back into slavery. Often they came with plantation owners from the Caribbean, like Pero who was brought to Bristol, England in 1783 by John Pinney, an owner of a sugar plantation on Nevis in the West Indies. Others arrived in Britain as purchases by (or gifts to) ship captains, but no matter how they were brought into Britain, having a black servant was a symbol of prestige.

The Somerset Case highlighted the ambiguity in the law. James Somerset was brought to England as an enslaved domestic worker by his owner, Charles Stewart. Somerset ran away and when recaptured his owner put him on a ship

Above left: Tax form for the City of Vicksburg, Mississippi, showing Benjamin Phillips paying $8, 40c for city tax in 1856, including slaves as taxable property.

Above right: This will was presented to the Probate Court and lists the property of Joseph C. Bursso, Wilcox County, Alabama, 25 February 1863 including domestic enslaved workers. The enslaved were split between the three heirs.

preparing to sail to Jamaica, returning him to slavery. The abolitionist Granville Sharp championed Somerset's case and got him removed from the ship before it sailed. In 1772 Lord Justice Mansfield ruled that Somerset needed to give his consent before being removed from Britain, and Somerset was set free. The judgement was misunderstood as people thought the ruling had freed enslaved workers, but this was not the case, since they had always been free under English and Welsh law.

Many slave-servants managed to gain their freedom in England and a few became well known. Ignatius Sancho (1729–80) was born on a slave ship and became a domestic servant in Britain and eventually owned his own grocery shop. Mary Prince was brought to London by her Bermudan owner and in 1828 fled from him and became a washerwoman, and with the aid of members of the Anti-Slavery Society wrote her memoirs, published in 1831.

RESISTANCE

With the rights of the enslaved being limited and freedom of movement non-existent it was not surprising that there were many acts of individual and group resistance. Rebellion or uprising in any country was of concern for all slave owners as it could inspire revolts or acts of disobedience anywhere where slavery existed. For this reason the authorities quashed any signs of disobedience brutally. It should be noted that on the one hand the authorities did all they could to prevent uprisings – however, when it suited them they also encouraged rebellion if it helped destabilise their enemies: during the American War of Independence the British encouraged the enslaved workers to run away from their owners and join the British forces, with the promise of freedom.

PASSIVE RESISTANCE
Passive resistance was the most common. This included feigning illness to avoid work, pretending not to understand instructions, breaking or losing tools and working slowly. It also included singing songs as they worked in the fields and teaching children about Africa, their traditions and previous rebellion leaders. Unfortunately, some took drastic action against themselves and their families; they took poisons to induce abortions and murdered their infants to save them from a life of enslavement. Any perceived passive resistance was dealt with harshly, as Mary Prince recalled: 'If we could not keep up with the rest of the gang of slaves, we were put in the stocks, and severely flogged the next morning.'

UPRISING AND REBELLION
In the Caribbean the most successful slave revolt occurred in Hispaniola, modern Haiti, and began in 1791. The rebellion started under the leadership of a religious man named Boukman, but eventually Toussaint L'Ouverture, a charismatic statesman, took over. The uprising was of such momentous importance to the region that the British, French and Spanish all sent forces to try to end the rebellion. L'Ouverture realised that success would only be

Opposite:
Rebel Maroon in
Suriname, 1770s.
Escaped slaves
formed Maroon
communities, and
these played an
important role in
the histories of
Brazil, Jamaica and
Suriname.

possible if his forces allied with one of the European powers who wanted the island. He chose France, a country that had just gone through its own revolution, and with their support he was able to govern. However, when Napoleon came to power in France he sent 20,000 troops to take back the country, and the former enslaved workers started a guerrilla war. L'Ouverture again made peace with the French, but was tricked, arrested and deported to France where he died in 1803. Jean-Jacques Dessalines continued the bloody war against the French and in 1803 Dessalines's forces were victorious and he became the leader of the new Republic.

There were other limited successes. Runaway slaves called 'Maroons' (from the Spanish word 'cimarrón' meaning 'wild') developed their own communities in Guyana, Suriname, Florida and Jamaica. In Jamaica, Spanish slaves who had escaped into the hills when Britain took control in 1655 fought against the British and helped slaves to escape. As the raids on plantations increased the British had to do something to end this defiance. The First Maroon War was led by Cudjoe and Nanny of the Maroons, the leaders of a highly organised community founded in the 1690s in the Back Rio Grande Valle. The British were unable to defeat the Maroons and the peace treaty of 1739 recognised the Maroons as free people and granted Nanny 500 acres of land from the Jamaican Government for herself and her people. In return the Maroons agreed to ally themselves with the Government of Jamaica against any invader and to hand over any runaway slaves. It was an uneasy truce and in 1795 the Second Maroon War broke out. In 1796 the British offered a peace treaty but reneged on their word by deporting the most troublesome Maroons to Sierra Leone, via Nova Scotia.

Vegetation on the Blue Mountains in Jamaica was so dense that it was easy for camouflaged Maroons to lie in wait for British soldiers.

Both: Sam Sharpe memorial, National Heroes Park, Kingston, Jamaica. Sharpe was leader of the 1832 uprising.

Most other rebellions failed. In Jamaica the final and largest uprising was the Baptist War of 1831–32, which began when Sam Sharpe, a Baptist preacher, led a general strike. It turned violent and 60,000 of Jamaica's 300,000 enslaved workers took part in a ten-day revolt. Two hundred and seven enslaved workers and fourteen whites were killed in the revolt and 340 people were executed for their involvement. Elsewhere in the Caribbean, Nanny Grigg set up militant action in 1816 at Simmons Plantation, Barbados, fighting for her belief that all humans are born free. In Matanzas province, Cuba in 1843, 'talking drums' called the rebels to battle and three enslaved workers, including the enslaved female Carlota, led the workers at the Triumvirato sugar plantations in a rebellion. Initially successful, the authorities took control and ended the uprising. Carlota was captured, tortured and killed, and the revolt later became known as 'Carlota's Rebellion'.

South America also saw many revolts. From the end of the sixteenth century Palmares, in northeastern Brazil, became a centre of resistance for escaped enslaved workers. Around 30,000 people lived in the region working small subsistence farms and raiding nearby plantations and towns for supplies. Military expeditions eventually defeated the rebels and in 1695 Zumbi, the leader, was captured and beheaded. In 1763 Cuffy (Kofi)

Brimstone Hill, St Kitts, W.I.
(The old Gibraltar of the West Indies)

Brimstone Hill, St Kitts, was one of many forts built to protect trade and prevent uprisings in the Caribbean. These forts are a testament to the enslaved labourers' construction skills and a sign of the control Europeans held over the enslaved.

led a slave revolt in the Dutch colony of Berbice, in modern-day Guyana. Cuffy and over 2,500 slaves held Berbice for ten months, but disagreements among the rebels and attacks by the Dutch led to Cuffy's suicide and the collapse of the rebellion. In Surinam between 1772 and 1777 the Dutch ran an expedition against the rebelling enslaved workers. The revolt was brutally brought to an end and the account of John Stedman (who had joined the expedition and recorded the horrors of the

RANAWAY from the subscriber, on the 30th July last, WALTER CALLEN-DER, an Apprentice to the Britannia and Pewter ware business. He is about 20 years of age, 5 feet 6 or 7 inches high, light complexion, and slender frame. All persons are hereby forbid harboring or trusting said Callender, on penalty of the law: no debts contracted by him, will be paid by the subscriber.　　　　　IRA COUCH. Meriden, Aug. 28, 1835.　　　　　4w*88

treatment of the enslaved) was used as evidence by the anti-slavery movement in Britain.

In the USA there were over two hundred slave revolts or conspiracies between 1600 and 1865, some being very well organised. In 1800 Gabriel Prosser recruited a thousand slaves and planned to march on Richmond, Virginia. Prosser was betrayed and he and many of his followers were executed. In 1822, Vesey (a free black man) and his followers planned to set fire to Charleston and kill the white families as they fled their houses. Before the fire could be lit a follower betrayed Vesey and he and the other leaders were hanged. When the full plans were revealed the southern slave owners were shocked by the extent and ingenuity of the plot.

The most successful revolt in the USA occurred in 1831 when Nat Turner, a slave preacher in Virginia, and seven followers entered his owner's home and killed the family. They moved from one farm to the next, killing all slave-owning whites they found and were joined by other enslaved workers. Eventually Turner, together with eighty of his followers, was intercepted by the militia. Turner escaped, and in the two months he evaded capture the militia and white vigilantes killed hundreds of slaves. Turner was eventually hanged.

$500 REWARD.

RANAWAY from the subscriber's plantation, Parish of Iberville, La., some time the latter part of March last, two negro men. JACOB, aged 25 or 28 years, very stout, heavy set with full round face, black complexion, 5 feet 7 or eight inches high, speaks very slow and precise when spoken to with an impediment in his speech. JIM, aged about 45 or 50 years, very black, 5 feet 9 or 10 inches high, speaks plain and affable when spoken to, with a very stern forbidding countenance. I will pay the above reward for their apprehension and delivery if taken in any one of the Western States, or I will pay two hundred dollars if taken either in Mississippi, Alabama or Louisiana.

s13 2t W   EDWARD MOORE.

N. B. As Jacob was purchased some two years since in New Orleans, where he had been living for 6 or 7 years in a brick yard, he may still be lurking about the city.

☞ The Cincinnati Weekly Republican will please give the above 4 insertions and charge this office.

Left and opposite: Runaway adverts (New Orleans *Picayune*, 1841, and *Columbia Register*, 1835). Success rates for escapees were low as trained hounds and ex-slaves chased down runaways and rewards were offered.

The big cities were not without their troubles. In 1712 twenty-five enslaved workers armed with guns and clubs burned down houses on the northern edge of New York City and killed nine people. Soldiers arrived and killed the rebels, and later executed eighteen participants in the rebellion. 1741 saw the New York Conspiracy, when thirty-one enslaved workers and four whites were executed as a result of rumours of a major slave rebellion in New York City. It is unclear whether there was a real rebellion planned or whether it was just the result of the city's paranoia.

ESCAPE

The occasional mass uprising was one thing but for the enslaved the easiest way to hurt their owner economically was to escape. Some escaped in groups, like in 1739 when around eighty armed enslaved workers ran away from South Carolina toward Spanish Florida (leading to the death of forty-four blacks and twenty-one whites when the militia fought with the escapees). Most, however, escaped in smaller groups or as individuals, like Harriet Jacobs who ran away from her owner in 1834 with a reward of $300 offered for her capture. Many of these escaping individuals needed assistance and in the USA this led to the development of the 'Underground Railroad', an informal process whereby those who opposed slavery aided the escaping enslaved. They provided food and hid them, often risking arrest or worse. The best-known railroad 'conductor' was Harriet Tubman who had escaped slavery in 1849. From 1851 Harriet made nineteen trips back to the south, helping over three hundred people escape to freedom in

Both: Punishment in Surinam, 1770s. There was no appeal process and the enslaved were at the whim of their owners.

Punishment of slaves in the USA.

the North, including her sisters, brothers and parents. She was a hero to the enslaved and a reward of $40,000 was offered for her arrest. Harriet was never caught and never lost a 'passenger', becoming known as the 'Moses of her people'.

Punishment of an enslaved woman on a Brazilian sugar plantation, 1845.

Olaudah Equiano,

or

EMANCIPATION

THE FOUNDER of the Quakers (the religious Society of Friends), George Fox (1624–91), was appalled at the treatment of the enslaved, which he saw first-hand during a visit to Barbados in 1671. He demanded that plantation owners should treat their workers better, yet stopped short of calling for emancipation. Later, in Britain in 1787, it was the Quakers who formed the Society for the Abolition of the Slave Trade, with a committee of nine Quakers along with Granville Sharp and Thomas Clarkson (both Anglicans), and William Wilberforce as their parliamentary spokesman. Leading African abolitionists in Britain, like Olaudah Equiano who had bought himself out of slavery, supported the society; and women, who made up ten per cent of the membership, raised awareness of the violation of family life under slavery.

Often the actions of the enslaved are overlooked when discussing emancipation, but through revolts they fought for their own rights and were probably the most influential people in the struggle for their freedom. They were not the passive kneeling people begging for their freedom depicted in Josiah Wedgwood's illustration. The anti-slavery movement believed that the successful slave revolt in Haiti and failed uprisings in Jamaica showed that an economy supported by enslaved labour could be unstable and expensive to protect, and it would be more profitable to end slavery and use employed labour.

THE BRITISH ANTI-SLAVERY MOVEMENT

In 1787 British abolitionists set up Freetown in Sierra Leone for repatriated and rescued Africans and as a new start in Africa for blacks in London who wanted to escape from the poverty they lived in. The first large group that was sent comprised thousands of enslaved workers who had escaped their owners and joined the British forces during the American War of Independence (1775–83). After Britain's defeat they had been moved to Nova Scotia and abandoned. British abolitionists wanted to see the promise of freedom honoured, so in 1792 John Clarkson, brother of Thomas Clarkson, organised their transportation to Sierra Leone.

Opposite:
Olaudah Equiano
(1745–97).

William Wilberforce (1759–1833).

One of the most important aspects of the British anti-slavery campaign was the population's support. It was the first major civil movement for human rights in Britain as consumers became aware that their enjoyment was gained at a cost: the exploitation of enslaved labour. In 1792 the West Indian sugar boycott started and at its peak at least 300,000 people had given up sugar, with grocers reporting sales falling by half. Other workers refused to make products to be used in the slave trade.

Even with the slave uprisings and public awareness nothing could happen without political pressure. Thomas Clarkson risked his life gathering evidence from British ports and his work aided William Wilberforce when he presented evidence of the horrors of the slave trade in parliamentary debates. In 1806 Lord Grenville formed a new government and argued that the slave trade was 'contrary to the principles of justice, humanity and sound policy'. In 1807 the Abolition

Below left: Josiah Wedgwood, potter and abolitionist, produced a ceramic cameo of a kneeling male slave in chains with the slogan 'Am I Not a Man and a Brother?' This image appeared on many anti-slavery items, including this 1795 English token.

Below right: American token (1838) showing the image of a kneeling woman, a design produced by Wedgwood's wife.

of the Slave Trade bill was passed with clear majorities in both the House of Commons and House of Lords, abolishing the transatlantic slave trade but not slavery itself.

Between 1808 and 1888 British Navy patrols freed 150,000 enslaved Africans from around 1,600 slave ships. Most of the Africans were freed back into Africa, mainly to Sierra Leone. However, 15,000 were freed into the Caribbean and affected the cultural development of countries like the Bahamas. Originally they worked under an apprenticeship of between seven and fourteen years, during which they should have been taught English, Christianity and a trade. As the employers of apprenticed labourers often failed to meet their obligations in educating the apprentices, and worked this cheap labour in conditions no better than slavery, apprenticeships were eventually reduced to six months or less. These liberated Africans became productive members of the workforce and developed their own communities, reinforcing African traditions.

Wilberforce believed slavery would gradually end once the African slave trade ceased. As this didn't happen protests to end slavery in British territories were renewed. The British Government implemented new laws to protect the enslaved but as these did not go far enough the Anti-Slavery Society was founded in 1823, with members including Clarkson and Wilberforce. Women were excluded from its leadership so the Birmingham

Below: Wilberforce Memorial Hall in Freetown, Sierra Leone c.1900.

Ladies Society for the Relief of Negro Slaves (becoming the Female Society for Birmingham) was formed in 1825 and by 1831 there were seventy-three anti-slavery women's organisations. Women activists such as Anne Knight and Elizabeth Heyrick were in favour of immediate abolition of slavery and in 1830 the Female Society for Birmingham submitted a resolution calling for an immediate end to slavery in the British colonies. At the National Conference the Anti-Slavery Society agreed to drop the words 'gradual abolition' from its title, and campaign for immediate abolition.

Some high-profile individuals believed abolitionists would bring the nation to ruin. Members of Parliament who had a vested interest in the Caribbean trade staunchly opposed abolition; the British royal family also sanctioned slavery. The great military hero of the day, Admiral Lord Nelson, had interests in sugar plantations in St Kitts and denounced 'the damnable doctrine of Wilberforce and his hypocritical allies', and said that he would fight to defend 'the just rights' of the West Indian planters. Their arguments had failed, as the abolitionists' case was much stronger.

Both: Baker's token (1795), commemorating the act to restrict Sunday working. Some British workers took advantage of the anti-slavery sentiment and used the evocative word 'slavery' to meet their own needs in trade disputes.

The abolitionists eagerly used the words of those who had been enslaved, for example Mary Prince who stated, 'I feel great sorrow when I hear some people in this country say that the slaves do not need better usage, and do not want to be free.' In 1833 the Government passed a bill outlawing slavery in British territories, and it became law on 1 August 1834. Slave owners received £20 million in compensation for the loss of their property, the enslaved workers – equivalent to £12 per slave. The enslaved workers gained no financial award or any land to call their own. Many were no better off as now their employers did not have to provide them with housing, clothing or land to produce crops, and many left the plantations in search of work and land.

Left: A token issued in Sierra Leone, 1814, recording the abolition of the slave trade by Britain in 1807.

In 1834 many British territories approved the introduction of a six-year apprenticeship to teach former slaves to be 'free people'. In truth it was a transition period for the plantation owners to find alternative workers, and the former enslaved were treated no better than before. The ineffectiveness of the system and campaigns against apprenticeship meant it ended on 1 August 1838, just four years after abolition.

Below: Liberated Africans just after their slave ship was captured.

Capture of a slaver
off the coast of
Cuba, 1858.

Birmingham Town
Hall, c.1900.
Between 1834 and
1838 the anti-
slavery movement
in Birmingham
lobbied for change
in the
apprenticeship
scheme at
meetings in the
newly opened
Town Hall.

The British anti-slavery movement did not end with emancipation in British territories. Slavery still existed around the world and the British and Foreign Anti-Slavery Society was formed on 17 April 1839, later to become Anti-Slavery International in 1990. In 1840, English Quaker Joseph Sturge organised the World Anti-Slavery Congress in London to unify anti-slavery groups in the UK and USA.

Above: Buxton Memorial commemorating the work of Thomas Foxwell Buxton and other abolitionists. It was removed from Parliament Square in 1940 and erected at its present position in Victoria Tower Gardens, London, in 1957.

Below: A token issued to commemorate the 1833 Act.

EMANCIPATION IN THE USA

Just as they had in Britain, the Quakers played a major part in the emancipation movement in the USA. In 1775 they formed the Society for the Relief of Free Negroes Unlawfully Held in Bondage, and by 1804 their work had helped abolish slavery in every northern state. American involvement in the transatlantic slave trade was made illegal in 1808, and by the 1830s the pressure on the southern states was so intense that anti-slavery literature was banned in the south and any teachers from the north who sympathised with the enslaved were expelled.

Some people in the north were concerned there would be an influx of cheap labour once slavery was abolished and during the 1820s and 1830s the American Colonization Society proposed returning American blacks to Africa. It had broad support and established the colony of Liberia in 1821–22. Over the next forty years it assisted thousands of former slaves and free blacks to move there, and abolitionists such as Henry Highland Garnet, born a slave in 1815, supported emigration to Mexico, Liberia and the West Indies, believing opportunities for freed slaves would be greater than in the USA.

On the other hand many freed or escaped enslaved people wanted to remain in the USA and became involved in the anti-slavery movement. Two of the most prominent were Frederick Douglass, an ex-slave who published

Frederick Douglass (1818–95) was a major voice in the anti-slavery campaign in the USA. He later turned his attention to women's suffrage.

This 1861 American illustration of John Bull, a national personification of Great Britain, suggests that Britain was not really interested in removing world slavery as they were not supporting the northern states against the southern states.

his own abolitionist newspaper, and Isabella Bomefree: freed from slavery in 1827, she changed her name to Sojourner Truth (meaning 'travelling preacher') and became one of America's foremost anti-slavery campaigners.

Even though many churches supported the abolitionist movement, not all did. When Daniel O'Connell, the Roman Catholic leader in Ireland, urged Irish-Americans to support abolition, many refused as they saw the newly freed enslaved competing for the same jobs as themselves. And although slavery was condemned by Pope Gregory XVI in 1839, the Catholic Church in America still seemed to support slaveholding interests.

In the 1830s William Lloyd Garrison led a campaign for 'immediate emancipation, gradually achieved', demanding that slave owners set up a system of emancipation. Most northerners favoured gradual and compensated emancipation but after 1849 demand for immediate emancipation grew. Many lobbied peacefully; however, some advocated violence. In 1859 John Brown raided the arsenal at Harper's Ferry and seized weapons for his insurrection. When the local slaves did not come to assist him the militia cut down Brown's men, killing eight of the twenty-two men. The captured men, including Brown, were tried and hanged.

Harriet Beecher Stowe, author of *Uncle Tom's Cabin*.

In 1851 Harriet Beecher Stowe's anti-slavery novel *Uncle Tom's Cabin*, inspired by the true story of escaped slave Josiah Henson, appeared in the anti-slavery journal, the *National Era*. The following year it was published as a book, selling over 300,000 copies in its first year. Frederick Douglass later stated, 'Its effect was amazing, instantaneous and universal', and thirty pro-slavery novels were published in an attempt to reverse public sympathies.

Eventually the tension between the Union (the northern states), which controlled the country, and the Confederates (the southern states), who wanted more autonomy, became too much. This friction led to a civil war (1861–65), with slavery becoming a focal point. By 1862, the Union was losing and their leader, Abraham Lincoln, announced that runaway enslaved workers joining his army would be freed, and, if they won, slavery would be abolished. On 1 January 1863 the Emancipation Proclamation freed all slaves, even though the war was still going on. Union victory in 1865 saw the 13th Amendment to the Constitution, stating: 'Neither slavery nor involuntary servitude, except as a punishment for crime whereof the party shall have been duly convicted, shall exist within the United States, or any place subject to their jurisdiction.'

Other parts of the New World came under pressure to end slavery. Many in Britain wanted to see emancipation in Cuba and Brazil, not only for moral

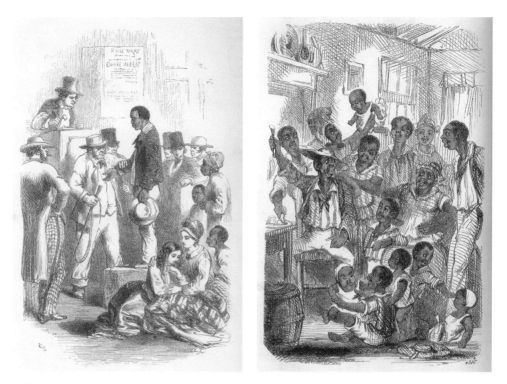

The above scenes are taken from the 1853 *Uncle Tom's Cabin* printed in England. Tom goes up for inspection (left) and Sam relates in the kitchen the particulars of Eliza's escape (right).

The debate over the American Civil War split many families.

Left: An enslaved worker tears up a map of America whilst representatives of the North and South look on. It illustrates the disunity in America that led to the Civil War.

Opposite top left: Abraham Lincoln Memorial, Washington.

Opposite top right: This statue of Abraham Lincoln in Washington shows one of the enslaved workers that he has helped to free kneeling at his feet.

Opposite bottom:
The Civil War showed the bravery of enslaved and free blacks as they fought in special black regiments.

reasons but also because the slave-produced sugar was cheaper than that from British colonies, causing economic problems in those territories. Cuba abolished slavery in 1886, and when in 1888 Pedro II abolished slavery, Brazil became the last nation in the Western Hemisphere to do so. Landowners, who had received no compensation, organised opposition to the monarchy, leading to the development of the Brazilian Republic in 1889.

Above: Celebrating news of emancipation, 1865. Abraham Lincoln is shown on the left, with Union soldiers on the right.

LEGACIES OF SLAVERY

RACISM

THE transatlantic slave trade created many legacies that are visible today in the Americas, Europe and Africa. The most obvious of these is racism. The trade was based on the principle that Africans and their descendents were inferior due to the colour of their skin. For nearly four hundred years British people were taught that a person's skin colour was important and that white was superior. However, not all saw it this way: Captain Phillips of the slave ship *Hannibal* stated in 1694, 'I can't think there is any intrinsick value in one colour more than another, nor that white is better than black, only we think it so, and are prone to judge favourably in our own case, as well as the blacks, who in odium of the colour, say, the devil is white, and so paint him.' This racism was more pronounced in the New World where people suffered further classification based upon the 'colour' of their parents.

Marcus Garvey (1887–1940), a Jamaican-born black nationalist who created the 'Back to Africa' movement in the United States and was an inspirational figure for later civil rights activists wrote, 'Black skin is not a badge of shame, but rather a glorious symbol of National greatness.' Racism is a difficult concept to alter and is still apparent in modern society. It is slowly being addressed by laws, education, and by the numerous black role models in politics, science, sports and entertainment.

WOMEN'S RIGHTS

One area that is constantly overlooked as a legacy of slavery is women's suffrage. One-fifth of all funds for the Anti-Slavery Society from 1823 to 1834 was raised by the numerous women's anti-slavery societies throughout Britain. Women were treated unequally by the male leaders and in 1826 Wilberforce wrote, 'For ladies to meet, to publish, to go from house to house stirring up petitions – these appear to me proceedings unsuited to the female character as delineated in Scripture. I fear its tendency would be to mix them in all the multiform warfare of political life.' These views riled many women but their priority was

Opposite:
The Parish Church of St Thomas in the Turks and Caicos Islands was built using enslaved workers.

My wife wont let me!!

Florence Kate Upton created this children's storybook character in 1895, based on a black-and-white minstrel doll. Popular in the first half of the twentieth century, Gollies later became a sign of overt racism and lost popularity.

the emancipation of the enslaved. Although excluded from the leadership, many working- and middle-class women were involved in the campaigns, boycotting slave-grown produce and writing anti-slave trade verses. Following the disbanding of the women's anti-slavery societies in the UK in 1833, women who had obtained experience in these societies turned their attention to other issues including the women's suffragette movement. The exclusion of women speakers at the 1840 International Slavery Conference in London generated a turning point for the women's suffragette movement in the UK and USA, and led to the development of formal suffragette organisations. Anne Knight, a British abolitionist, was furious and established the first association for women's suffrage in Britain in 1851; meanwhile the American delegates Elizabeth Stanton and Lucretia Mort led the women's rights movement in the USA.

ARCHITECTURE

There are also physical legacies of the slave trade. In the Americas many ruined buildings stand as a monument to the period of slavery. Many are old plantation sites but there are also structures such as administrative buildings, large houses and churches that are a testament to the skilled enslaved labour that built them. In Britain many large estate buildings were constructed using proceeds made from the slave trade or the use of enslaved labour on plantations. Some city landscapes, like Bristol, Liverpool and parts of London such as West India Docks, were also developed using money raised through slavery. As James Baille, a pro-slavery Member of Parliament whose family had profited from slavery stated, in 1830, 'Bristol owes ALL her prosperity, nay, her existence to her commerce with the West Indies.' These ports grew to build the slave ships, to manage the cargoes being taken out to trade for slaves and to house the imported cargoes from the Caribbean. At the same time fortunes made from the slave trade and from crops produced by the enslaved enabled Britain to build up a vast wealth. It was this wealth that was invested in the British economy and played a major role in the Industrial Revolution. This was the foundation on which Britain built her Empire.

BUSINESS AND FINANCE

In these cities the slave trade and associated business activities led to the formation of many companies to sustain it. These included financial organisations to insure businesses and slave ships, and to underwrite the developing companies, laying the foundations of the present well-known

'Crap at Coonville'. Racist images and words appeared in many products, which are now outlawed. There are still products promoted by the stereotypical African American such as Aunt Jemima and Uncle Ben: 'Uncle' and 'Aunt' were titles used to address older enslaved workers.

This administrative building in the Bahamas was built by slave labour.

Statue of Edward Colston (1636–1721), by John Cassidy (1895), located at Colston Avenue, Bristol, and a detail of one of the plaques on the base of the statue. Local people have made their feelings known by painting 'blood' dripping from his name.

banking and insurance institutions. There are also numerous reminders of the slave owners themselves: these reminders often appear as street names such as Penny Lane in Liverpool, made famous in the 1960s Beatles's song, which was named after James Penny, an eighteenth century slave ship owner. There are also statues of abolitionists and of those who prospered from the slave trade. In the latter case are people like Edward Colston whose statue stands in Bristol. He was a famous philanthropist who helped develop the city of Bristol, but his wealth came through his involvement in trading sugar from St Kitts and as an official of the Royal African Company, which monopolised the slave trade from Africa at the end of the seventeenth century.

CULTURAL DIVERSITY

The positive legacies of the African diaspora include diversity of culture and cultural interaction spreading throughout the Americas and Europe. Due to recent migration, access to these traditions has increased. Probably the most recognisable cultural legacy is the music and in particular the African influences in rhythm. Some types of music can trace their roots back to slavery; for example, the drums used in Samba music were tolerated by Brazilian slave owners, whereas US slave owners feared the use of drums when used for communication. Another example of West African influence is the storytelling tradition, including characters like Anansi the Spider and B'rabbi, a wily rabbit better known today as Brer Rabbit or Bugs Bunny.

Many of these storytelling characters undertake mischievous adventures that end with a moral, and were common in enslaved communities.

Cultural legacy is also illustrated by carnival, masquerade and junkanoo performances, which are now common throughout the Caribbean, USA and Europe. These have direct roots in Africa. In 1811 Dowson, a Methodist missionary, wrote of the celebrations in the Turks and Caicos Islands, 'I never before witnessed such a Christmas Day; the negroes have been beating their tambourines and dancing the whole day and now between eight and nine o'clock they are pursuing their sport as hotly as ever.'

Europeans tried to justify slavery by claiming it was a means to bring the Africans and their descendants into Christianity. This meant Christianity became a major part of enslaved workers' lives, but it was adapted by them to include their African beliefs, often associating their gods with the personae of Christian saints. At the same time, slave owners feared organised religion as it encouraged individual thought and allowed slaves to gather in large numbers. Methodism and Baptism became the denominations of choice for many of the enslaved, not Anglicanism or Catholicism, as they were less formal and welcomed all to participate in the ceremonies, including as lay preachers. Where African culture was allowed to become more ingrained many enslaved kept their African religions and in places like Brazil these religions still have millions of followers.

One of the most outstanding decorative forms of Ashanti crafts is the Kente cloth, a visual representation of history, philosophy, ethics, oral literature and moral, religious, and political ideology.

Mask wearer in the
Congo, c.1900 and
a modern
junkanoo/carnival
performance in the
Turks and Caicos
Islands, West
Indies.

The legacy of slavery in the Caribbean is not just an African one. The ethnic diversity in the Caribbean increased following the move of many former enslaved workers away from the plantations to build new lives. This labour shortage on the plantations in Trinidad, Guyana, Suriname and Jamaica was met with the importation of over half a million indentured labourers mostly from China and India. The indentured labourers worked for a fixed number of years for the promise of their own land but were treated no better than slaves and following a campaign in India by Mahatma Gandhi, Britain outlawed the use of indentured labour in 1917.

A LASTING LEGACY

One of the largest legacies of the slave trade is the situation in Africa today. The transatlantic slave trade depleted the African continent of many of its young adults and stalled its development. At the same time the slave trade in Africa was just the beginning of the colonial development of the continent and with the end of the European slave trade, European powers fought over Africa's natural resources. Often disguised as expeditions to oust slave traders, or to build alliances to protect African kings, Britain started to colonise large parts of West Africa and consolidated their control of the Gold Coast, dominating the region and exploiting cocoa, gold, timber and palm oil. At the Berlin Conference (1884–85) European countries split the continent into almost fifty European colonies, ignoring the people, cultures and traditional tribal boundaries. It is these artificial boundaries created by the Europeans that are blamed for many of the problems in Africa today.

Slavery was not assigned to the history books when the European nations outlawed it in their territories. The slave trade continued as a lucrative economic enterprise and as a means of keeping control over people, most notably in the Congo (ending in 1909) and Zanzibar (formally ending in 1873

Indentured labour in Jamaica, c.1900.

The British anti-slavery campaigners have continued to fight for their cause. In the early 1900s they fought to end slavery in the Congo.

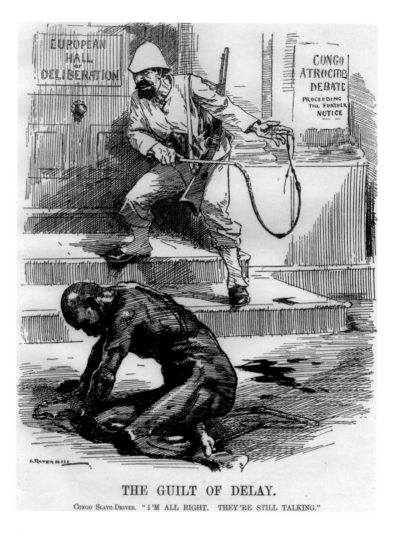

THE GUILT OF DELAY.

Congo Slave-Driver. "I'M ALL RIGHT. THEY'RE STILL TALKING."

but continuing into the twentieth century). More recently the situation in Darfur, Sudan, that came to public attention in 2003 highlighted that modern conflicts not only displaced millions of people, but also opens the local population to all sorts of abuse, including enslavement.

The Universal Declaration of Human Rights of 1948 states that 'No one shall be held in slavery or servitude; slavery and the slave trade shall be prohibited in all their forms'. However, in 2005 it was estimated there were over 12 million enslaved people in the world. What the end of the transatlantic slave trade has shown, as well as the end of slavery in the Congo and Zanzibar, was how public pressure and the role of individuals can bring about political

Left: The atrocities in the Belgian Congo (ended in 1909) raised the attention of the world to the fact that slavery was still happening. Campaigns in Europe and the USA forced the situation to change.

Left: An anti-slavery march in Birmingham, England in 2007. The march was led by an actor dressed as Olaudah Equiano and included a relative of Jospeh Sturge, who had led the campaign at Birmingham Town Hall in the 1830s to end the apprenticeship scheme.

changes. Today these challenges are being met not only by Anti Slavery International but also by those people who lobby governments to encourage greater financial support, aid, expertise, education and opportunities to areas where enslaved labour is used.

Right: Slavery was outlawed in Zanzibar in 1873 and the Great Slave Market closed down. However, slavery still existed in the region, as shown by this image of an escaping enslaved African, dated c.1910.

BIBLIOGRAPHY

ACCOUNTS OF THE ENSLAVED

Eickelmann, Christine and Small, David. *Pero: The Life of a Slave in Eighteenth-Century Bristol*. Redcliffe Press, Bristol, 2004.

Ferguson, Moira. *History of Mary Prince, A West Indian Slave*. University of Michigan Press, 1996.

Gates, Henry Louis. *Classic Slave Narratives*. Penguin Books, London, 1987.

Lester, Julius. *To Be a Slave*. Penguin Books, London, 1998.

Nazer, Mende and Lewis, Damien. *Slave*. Virago Press, London, 2004.

GENERAL BOOKS ON SLAVERY

Bailey, Anne C. *African Voices of the Atlantic Slave Trade*. Ian Randle Publishers, Jamaica, 2007.

Coules, Victoria. *The Trade: Bristol and the Transatlantic Slave Trade*. Birlinn, Edinburgh, 2007.

Curtin, Philip D. *The Rise and Fall of the Plantation Complex*. Cambridge University Press, Cambridge, 1998.

Everett, Susanne. *History of Slavery: An Illustrated History of the Monstrous Evil*. Chartwell Books Inc., New Jersey, 2006.

Foster, Nadia. *Out of Slavery*. Redcliffe Publishing, Bristol, 2004.

Hague, William. *William Wilberforce: The Life of the Great Anti-Slave Trade Campaigner*. HarperCollins, London, 2007.

Harms, Robert. *The Diligent*. Basic Books, New York, 2002.

Hatt, Christine. *Slavery from Africa to the Americas*. Evans Brothers Limited, London, 2007.

Hochschild, Adam. *Bury the Chains: The British Struggle to Abolish Slavery*. Macmillan, London, 2005.

Kalman, Bobbie. *Life on a Plantation*. Crabtree Publishing, Oxford, 1997.

Klein, Herbert S. *The Atlantic Slave Trade*. Cambridge University Press, Cambridge, 1999.

McEvedy, Colin. *The Penguin Atlas of African History*. Penguin, London, 1995.

McKissack, Patricia C. and Frederick L. *Rebels against Slavery: American Slave Revolts*. Scholastic, New York, 1999.

Martin, S. I. *Britain's Slave Trade*. Macmillan, London, 1999.

Monaghan, Tom. *The Slave Trade*. Evans Brothers Limited, London, 2002.

Reddie, Richard S. *Abolition! The Struggle to Abolish Slavery in the British Colonies*. Lion Hudson, Oxford, 2007.

St Clair, William. *The Grand Slave Emporium: Cape Coast Castle and the British Slave Trade*. Profile Books, London, 2007.

Saunders, Gail. *Slavery in the Bahamas, 1648–1838*. Nassau Guardian, Nassau, 1995.

Shepherd, Verene A. *Working Slavery, Pricing Freedom*. James Currey
    Publishers, Oxford, 2002.

Svalesen, Leif. *The Slave Ship Fredensborg*. Indiana University Press,
    Indiana, 2000.

Thomas, Hugh. *The Slave Trade: The Story of the Atlantic Slave Trade 1440–
    1870*. Simon and Schuster, New York, 1999.

Thomas, Velma Maia. *Lest We Forget*. Crown Publishers, New York, 2001.

Thomas, Velma Maia. *No Man Can Hinder Me: The Journey from Slavery to
    Emancipation through Song*. Crown Publishers, New York, 1997.

Walvin, James. *Questioning Slavery*. Ian Randle Publishers, Jamaica, 1997.

Walvin, James. *The Slave Trade*. Sutton Publishing Limited, Stroud, 1999.

Ward, W. E. F. *The Royal Navy and the Slavers: The Suppression of the Atlantic
    Slave Trade*. Pantheon Books, New York, 1968.

WEBSITES

International Slavery Museum, Liverpool:
    www.liverpoolmuseums.org.uk/ism

The legacy of the slave ship *Trouvadore*, wrecked in 1841:
    www.slaveshiptrouvadore.com

Resource for educators: www.understandingslavery.com

MOVIES AND TV

Amazing Grace (2007). Based on the story of William Wilberforce and his
    fight for abolition.

Amistad (1997). Based on the true story of the slave revolt on board the
    slave ship *Amistad*.

Burn (1969). Fictional account of a Caribbean slave revolt.

Roots (1977). TV series dramatising the story of Kunte Kinte, ancestor of
    the author Alex Haley.

INDEX